Clowns Do, Clowns Don't
Loonette's Book of Manners

Clowns Do, Clowns Don't

Loonette 's Book of Manners

Written by **Gavin Jackson**

Illustrated by **Pat Paris**

ALEXANDRIA,
VIRGINIA

Sleepyhead

When Loonette the clown gets up in the morning
and sees her best friend, Molly, what should she do?

Clowns DON'T say, "Get out of bed, lazy little clown!"
Clowns DO say, "Good morning!"

Who's the first person you usually see in the morning?

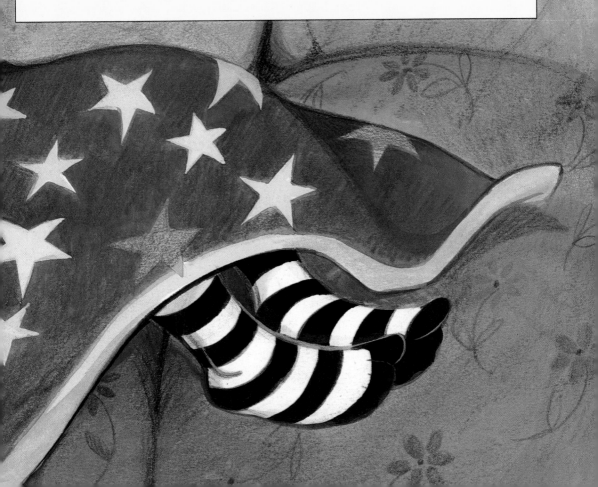

Elbow Room

When Loonette is doing her exercises and bumps into someclown, what should she do?

Clowns DON'T say, "Get outta my way!"
Clowns DO say, "Excuse me, please."

What other times might you bump into someone?

How Does That Grab You?

When Loonette is ready to eat,
what should she do?

Clowns DON'T stand and grab food off the table.

Clowns DO sit down and put a napkin
in their lap. They use a spoon—or a fork—
to help them eat.

What is your favorite food to eat for breakfast?

You Said a Mouthful

When Loonette is eating and wants to talk with someclown, what should she do?

Clowns DON'T talk with a mouth full of food.

Clowns DO chew with their mouth closed.
They talk when they have
no food left in their mouth.

What do you talk about at the table?

"Oops!"

When one clown sees another fall down,
what should she do?

Clowns DON'T laugh and ask if he's had a nice trip.
Clowns DO ask if they can help him get up.

Has anyone ever helped you when you fell?

"Kitty Did It!"

If something breaks by accident, what should a clown do? Clowns DON'T fib and blame the cat. Clowns DO tell the truth and say, "I'm sorry."

Did you ever break anything by accident?

"You're the Best!"

When someclown tells Loonette,
"You dance nicely," what should she do?

Clowns DON'T feel embarrassed.
It's nice to get a compliment!
Clowns DO say, "Thank you."

What are some things you do well?

Wait Your Turn

When someclown is having a snack and
another clown wants one too, what should she do?
Clowns DON'T grab.

Clowns DO ask, "Please, may I have one?"
When they are given the snack, they say, "Thank you."

What are your favorite snacks?

You Don't Say

When others are talking and someclown wants
to say something, what should she do?

Clowns DON'T interrupt. But if it's very important,
clowns DO say, "Excuse me," and tell what is so
important that they can't wait. Otherwise,
clowns DO wait their turn to speak.

What are some things that might be important enough for you to interrupt someone?

"Ready or Not, Here I Come!"

Before one clown comes to stay with another, what should she do?

Clowns DON'T just show up with their suitcases.

Clowns DO call ahead of time and say they're coming.

Who do you like to go visit?

"It's Mine!"

When the Dustbunnies are playing, what should they do?

Clowns DON'T fight over a toy.

Clowns DO share toys. They take turns so they can have fun together.

What toys do you like to play with?

"Gesundheit!"
When Loonette has to sneeze or cough,
what should she do?

Clowns DON'T sneeze or cough
in someclown's face.

Clowns DO cover their nose when they sneeze,
and their mouth when they cough.
Clowns always use a tissue to blow or wipe
their nose.

How do you feel when you have a cold?

Who Made This Big Mess?

When Loonette is finished
playing with her toys,
what should she do?

Clowns DON'T leave them
on the floor for other clowns
to trip over.
Clowns DO pick them up
and put them away where
they belong.

Where do you keep your toys?

Water, Water Everywhere

When someclown takes a bath,
what should she do?

Clowns DON'T
splash water in
another clown's face
or out of the tub.
Clowns DO wash
and play and have fun.

What do you like to do in the tub?

Shhh!
When someclown is trying to sleep,
what should other clowns do?

Clowns DON'T make a lot of noise.
Clowns DO try to be as quiet as a mouse.

What kind of noises sometimes keep you awake?

Nighty-night

When it's bedtime,
what does a clown do?

Clowns DON'T try to stay up past a clown's bedtime.
Clowns DO snuggle up and close their eyes.

Just like you, little clown.
Good night.